Puddle Wonderful

Poems to Welcome Spring

The time of the singing of birds is come
and the voice of the turtle
is heard in our land.

King Solomon, from Song of Songs

A Random House PICTUREBACK®

Grateful acknowledgment is made to the following for permission to reprint the copyrighted material listed below:

Atheneum Publishers, an imprint of Macmillan Publishing Company, for "Weird!" from *If I Were in Charge of the World and Other Worries* by Judith Viorst. Copyright © 1981 by Judith Viorst. Reprinted by permission of the publisher. BookStop Literary Agency for: "Hurrah for Spring Mud" by Judith Kinter. Copyright © 1990 by Judith Kinter. "Spring Cleaning" by Dee Lillegard. Copyright © 1991 by Dee Lillegard. Reprinted by permission of BookStop Literary Agency for the authors. Judith Ciardi for the excerpt from "The Easter Bunny" by John Ciardi. Copyright © 1985 by John Ciardi. Curtis Brown Ltd. for "We're Racing, Racing down the Walk" by Phyllis McGinley. Copyright © 1959, 1960 by Phyllis McGinley; copyright renewed © 1987 by Mrs. Richard Blake, 1988 by Patricia Blake. Greenwillow Books, a division of William Morrow & Company, for "The Court Jester's Last Stand" from *The Sheriff of Rottenshot* by Jack Prelutsky. Copyright © 1982 by Jack Prelutsky. Reprinted by permission of the publisher. HarperCollins Publishers for: "I Will Be Walking" from *Birds* by Arnold Adoff. Copyright © 1982 by Arnold Adoff. "Spring" from *Dogs & Dragons, Trees & Dreams* by Karla Kuskin. Copyright © 1980 by Karla Kuskin. The second stanza from "The Spring Wind" from *River Winding: Poems by Charlotte Zolotow.* Copyright © 1970 by Charlotte Zolotow. Reprinted by permission of HarperCollins Publishers. Margaret Hillert for "And Suddenly Spring" and "How It Happens." Used by permission of the author, who controls all rights. Paul Janeczko for "Spring." Copyright © 1991 by Paul Janeczko. Used by permission of the author, who controls all rights. Bobbi Katz for "It's Time for Spring," copyright © 1991, and "Spring Is," copyright © 1979. Used by permission of the author, who controls all rights. Alfred A. Knopf, Inc., for: "April Rain Song." Copyright 1932 by Alfred A. Knopf, Inc., and renewed 1960 by Langston Hughes. Reprinted from *The Dream Keeper and Other Poems* by Langston Hughes by permission of the publisher. British rights exclusive of Canada administered by Harold Ober Associates. "May" from *A Child's Calendar* by John Updike. Copyright © 1965 by John Updike and Nancy Burkert. Reprinted by permission of Alfred A. Knopf, Inc. Constance Levy for "Tree Coming Up" from *I'm Going to Pet a Worm Today and Other Poems,* published by Margaret K. McElderry Books, an imprint of Macmillan Publishing Company. Copyright © 1991 by Constance Kling Levy. Used by permission of the author. Liveright Publishing Corporation for "in Just" and the phrase "Puddle Wonderful" from the poem from *Tulips and Chimneys* by E. E. Cummings, edited by George James Firmage. Copyright 1923, 1925 and renewed 1951, 1953 by E. E. Cummings. Copyright © 1973, 1976 by the Trustees for the E. E. Cummings Trust. Copyright © 1973, 1976 by George James Firmage. Grafton Books, a division of HarperCollins Publishers Ltd., administers rights in the United Kingdom. MGA of Canada for "The Muddy Puddle" from *Garbage Delight* by Dennis Lee. Published by Macmillan of Canada. Copyright © 1977 by Dennis Lee. Penguin Books U.S.A. Inc. for "Robin" from *A Hippopotamusn't* by J. Patrick Lewis. Copyright © 1990 by J. Patrick Lewis. Reprinted by permission of the publisher, Dial Books for Young Readers. Mona R. Reeves for "Tell Me, Robin." Copyright © 1990 by Mona R. Reeves. Used by permission of the author, who controls all rights. Marian Reiner for: "Is It Robin O'Clock" from *Blackberry Ink* by Eve Merriam. Copyright © 1985 by Eve Merriam. "Forsythia Bush" from *I Thought I Heard the City* by Lilian Moore. Copyright © 1969 by Lilian Moore. Reprinted by permission of Marian Reiner for the authors. Mary Chute Smith for "Spring Rain" from *Rhymes About the City* by Marchette Chute. Copyright 1946 by Macmillan Co. Copyright renewed 1974 by E.P. Dutton. Reprinted by permission of Mary Chute Smith. Dorothy Brown Thompson for "Arbor Day," published first in *Story Parade* and copyright reassigned to Dorothy Brown Thompson. Used with permission of the author.

Library of Congress Cataloging-in-Publication Data
Puddle wonderful : poems to welcome spring / selected by Bobbi Katz ; illustrated by Mary Morgan.
p.   cm.—(Random House pictureback) Summary: A collection of poems about the many aspects of spring and spring holidays, by such poets as E.E. Cummings, Eve Merriam, Jack Prelutsky, Lilian Moore, and Dennis Lee. ISBN 0-679-81493-0 (trade)—ISBN 0-679-91493-5 (GLB) 1. Spring—Juvenile poetry. 2. Children's poetry. 3. Poetry—Collections. [1. Spring—Poetry. 2. Poetry—Collections.] I. Katz, Bobbi. II. Morgan, Mary, ill. PN6109.97.P84 1992 808.81'933—dc20 91-8066

Manufactured in the United States of America   10 9 8 7 6 5 4 3 2 1

Puddle Wonderful

Poems to Welcome Spring

selected by Bobbi Katz
illustrated by Mary Morgan

Random House 🏠 New York

Is It Robin O'Clock?

Is it robin o'clock?
Is it five after wing?
Is it quarter to leaf?
Is it nearly time for spring?

Is it grass to eleven?
Is it flower to eight?
Is it half-past snowflake?
Do we still have to wait?

Eve Merriam

It's Time for Spring

My sweater's tight and itchy.
My snow pants are too small.
Last week I lost a mitten.
I can't find my scarf at all!

My woolen socks have lost their toes.
My boots have lost their tread.
And I have lost the love I had
for words like "skis" and "sled"!

But…my fishing rod still fits.
And…my baseball bat still hits.
I have a kite that wants to fly.
So…Winter, call it quits!

Bobbi Katz

March

A blue day,
a blue jay
and a good beginning.

One crow,
melting snow—
spring's winning!

Elizabeth Coatsworth

Spring

A breezy ballerina
dances over foggy fields
as the icy bear of winter
melts away.

Paul B. Janeczko

I Will Be Walking

up and down
the
driveway this late march
morning

and
a cool wind
still from the north

but a warm sun
and
o
what
seeds were
under
the
winter
snows

Arnold Adoff

The March Wind

I come to work as well as play;
    I'll tell you what I do;
I whistle all the live-long day,
    "Woo-oo-oo-oo! Woo-oo!"

I toss the branches up and down
    And shake them to and fro,
I whirl the leaves in flocks of brown,
    And send them high and low.

I throw the twigs upon the ground,
    The frozen earth I sweep;
I blow the children round and round
    And wake the flowers from sleep.

Anonymous

And Suddenly Spring

The winds of March were sleeping.
I hardly felt a thing.
The trees were standing quietly.
It didn't seem like spring.
Then suddenly the winds awoke
And raced across the sky.
They bumped right into April,
Splashing springtime in my eye.

Margaret Hillert

from **The Spring Wind**

The wind I love the best
comes gently after rain
smelling of spring and growing things
brushing the world with feathery wings
while everything glistens, and everything sings
in the spring wind
after the rain.

Charlotte Zolotow

Tell Me, Robin

Robin, robin, tell me why
I must walk, but you can fly.
What? You think you'd like it here?
You would trade me for a year?

Yes, I've thought of trading, too.
Tell me, just what do you do?
Well, I know you chirp and sing.
Oh, your job's announcing spring?

What? A worm? No! Thank you, though!
Want some gum? Some candy? No?
Play a game? Or watch TV?
Sorry, bugs aren't food for me....

Do you like it, what you do?
Good. I like who I am, too.
I agree. This way's just fine.
You do your thing. I'll do mine.

Mona Rabun Reeve

Robin

Suddenly Spring wings
into the backyard, ready
to play tug-of-worm.

J. Patrick Lewis

Spring Is

Spring is when
        the morning sputters like
bacon
            and
                your
                    sneakers
                        run
                            down
                                the
                                    stairs
so fast you can hardly keep up with them,
and
spring is when
            your scrambled eggs
                jump
                    off
                        the
                            plate
and turn into a million daffodils
trembling in the sunshine.

Bobbi Katz

There Is Joy

There is joy in
Feeling the warmth
Come to the great world
And seeing the sun
Follow its old footprints.

Eskimo

The Crocus

The golden crocus reaches up
To catch a sunbeam in her cup.

Walter Crane

In Just

in Just-
spring   when the world is mud-
luscious the little
lame balloonman

whistles   far   and wee

and eddieandbill come
running from marbles and
piracies and it's
spring

when the world is puddle-wonderful

the queer
old balloonman whistles
far   and   wee
and bettyandisbel come dancing

from hop-scotch and jump-rope and

it's
spring
and
the

goat-footed

balloonMan   whistles
far
and
wee

e e cummings

The Muddy Puddle

I am sitting
In the middle
Of a rather Muddy
Puddle,
With my bottom
Full of bubbles
And my rubbers
Full of Mud,

While my jacket
And my sweater
Go on slowly
Getting wetter
As I very
Slowly settle
To the Bottom
Of the Mud.

And I find that
What a person
With a puddle
Round his middle
Thinks of mostly
In the muddle
Is the Muddi-
Ness of Mud.

Dennis Lee

Hurray for Spring Mud

My sisters pick buttercups bursting with spring;
My brothers chase mayflies while mockingbirds sing;
My friends splash in puddles and brooklets that flood;
But *I* love that swishable, squishable mud!

It chocolates my fingers, my knees, and my toes;
It makes mud pies to sun-bake and mud balls to throw.
Let others go wild about bird, bee, and bud;
Just give me my swishable, squishable mud!

Judith Kinter

We're Racing, Racing down the Walk

We're racing, racing down the walk,
Over the pavement and round the block.
We rumble along till the sidewalk ends—
Felicia and I and half our friends.
Our hair flies backward. It's whish and whirr!
She roars at me and I shout at her
As past the porches and garden gates
We rattle and rock
On our roller skates.

Phyllis McGinley

Forsythia Bush

There is nothing
quite
like the sudden
light

of
forsythia
that
one morning
without warning

explodes
into yellow
and
startles the street
into spring.

Lilian Moore

Spring Rain

The storm came up so very quick
    It couldn't have been quicker.
I should have brought my hat along,
    I should have brought my slicker.

My hair is wet, my feet are wet,
    I couldn't be much wetter.
I fell into a river once
    But this is even better.

Marchette Chute

Rain

Rain on the green grass
And rain on the tree,
And rain on the housetop,
But not upon me.

Anonymous

April Rain Song

Let the rain kiss you.
Let the rain beat upon your head with silver
    liquid drops.
Let the rain sing you a lullaby.

The rain makes still pools on the sidewalk.
The rain makes running pools in the gutter.
The rain plays a little sleep-song on our roof at
    night—
And I love the rain.

Langston Hughes

The Court Jester's Last Report to the King

Oh sire! My sire! your castle's on fire,
I fear it's about to explode,
a hideous lizard has eaten the wizard,
the prince has turned into a toad.

Oh sire! Good sire! there's woe in the shire,
fierce trolls are arriving in force,
there are pirates in port, monstrous ogres at court,
and a dragon has melted your horse.

Oh sire! Great sire! the tidings are dire,
a giant has trampled the school,
your army has fled, there are bees in your bed
and your nose has come off......APRIL FOOL!

Jack Prelutsky

Spring Cleaning

Furniture shifted,
rugs lifted,
cushions whacked,
pillows smacked.
Scrubbing brushes whizzing by
while the feather dusters fly.
Busy mop,
dizzy broom,
vacuum cleaner roaring—
ZOOM!
Help! It's heading for…
my room.

Dee Lillegard

Spring

I'm shouting
I'm singing
I'm swinging through trees
I'm winging sky-high
With the buzzing black bees.
I'm the sun
I'm the moon
I'm the dew on the rose.
I'm a rabbit
Whose habit
Is twitching his nose.
I'm lively
I'm lovely
I'm kicking my heels.
I'm crying "Come dance"
to the freshwater eels.
I'm racing through meadows
Without any coat
I'm a gamboling lamb
I'm a light leaping goat
I'm a bud
I'm a bloom
I'm a dove on the wing.
I'm running on rooftops
And welcoming spring!

Karla Kuskin

Weird

My sister Stephanie's in love.
(I thought she hated boys.)
My brother had a yard sale and
Got rid of all his toys.
My mother started jogging, and
My dad shaved off his beard.
It's spring—and everyone but me
Is acting really weird.

Judith Viorst

from **The Easter Bunny**

There once was an egg that felt funny.
It was chocolate brown, and got runny
    When a clucky old hen
    Sat to hatch it, and when
She was done, what popped out was—a bunny!

Said the hen, looking down, "Well, I say!
You're a strange looking chick! But please stay
    Till you learn to say *peep*."
    "There's a date I must keep,"
Said the bunny, and hip-hopped away.

John Ciardi

How It Happens

The wink of a pink and shining eye,
The swish of a mischievous tail,
The jerk of a perky nose held high,
The flight over hill and dale,
The rush through the hush of Easter Eve,
The pause of a paw, and then
The Easter basket beside the door
And Easter gladness again.

Margaret Hillert

from **A Shropshire Lad**

Loveliest of trees, the cherry now
Is hung with bloom along the bough,
And stands about the woodland ride
Wearing white for Eastertide.

A. E. Housman

Arbor Day

To plant a tree! How small the twig,
And I beside it—very big.
A few years pass; and now the tree
Looks down on very little me.
A few years more—it is so high
Its branches seem to touch the sky.
I did not know that it would be
So vast a thing to plant a tree.

Dorothy Brown Thompson

Tree Coming Up

A shoot, a shoot,
A greenish boot
Kicks open the door
Of the acorn house.

A split, a crack, a baby oak
Begins to push and stretch and poke
By a worm at home in a tunnel bed,

Past ants at work,
Past beetle nooks,

Through earth as rich as brown nut-bread
TREE COMING UP—LOOK OUT AHEAD!

Constance Levy

May

Now children may
   Go out of doors,
Without their coats,
   To candy stores.

The apple branches
   And the pear
May float their blossoms
   Through the air,

And Daddy may
    Get out his hoe
To plant tomatoes
    In a row,

And, afterwards,
    May lazily
Look at some baseball
    On TV.

                        John Updike

You, Whose Day It Is

You, whose day it is, make it beautiful.
Get out your rainbow colors,
So it will be beautiful.

Nootka